# FRANCE

Alice Harman

WAYLAND

**Get your paws on this fantastic new mega-series from Wayland!**

Join our Fact Cat on a journey of fun learning about every subject under the sun!

First published in 2014 by Wayland
© Wayland 2014

Wayland
Hachette Children's Books
338 Euston Road
London NW1 3BH

Wayland Australia
Level 17/207 Kent Street
Sydney NSW 2000

 Produced for Wayland by
White-Thomson Publishing Ltd
www.wtpub.co.uk
+44 (0) 843 208 7460

Editor: Alice Harman
Design: Rocket Design (East Anglia) Ltd
Fact Cat illustrations: Shutterstock/Julien Troneur
Other illustrations: Stefan Chabluk
Consultant: Kate Ruttle

A catalogue for this title is available from the British Library

ISBN: 978 0 7502 8212 3
ebook ISBN: 978 0 7502 8828 6

Dewey Number: 944-dc23

10 9 8 7 6 5 4 3 2 1

Wayland is a division of Hachette Children's Books,
an Hachette UK company.
www.hachette.co.uk

Printed and bound in China

Picture and illustration credits:
Alamy: Art Kowalsky 6, age footstock 14, Hemis 16;
Chabluk, Stefan 4; Dreamstime: Katarzyna Mazurowska 7,
Gordon Bell 8; Shutterstock: Sailorr 5, Ilona Ignatova 10,
Irina Kuzmina 11, bonchan 13, ErickN 17, Eoghan McNally
18; Jose Ignacio Soto cover; Thinkstock: ikick 9, zhuzhu
12, Christian Musat 15, Razvan 1 & 19, photos.com 20 & 22;
Wikimedia 20.

Every effort has been made to clear copyright.
Should there be any inadvertent omission,
please apply to the publisher for rectification.

The author, Alice Harman, is a writer and editor specialising in children's educational publishing.

The consultant, Kate Ruttle, is a literacy expert and SENCO, and teaches in Suffolk.

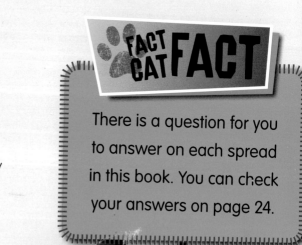

**FACT CAT FACT**

There is a question for you to answer on each spread in this book. You can check your answers on page 24.

# CONTENTS

# WELCOME TO FRANCE

France is a country in western Europe. Around 66 million people live there. It is the third largest country in Europe, after Russia and Ukraine.

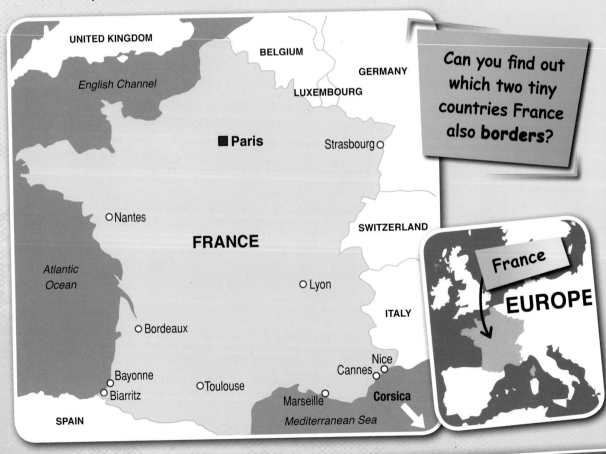

UNITED KINGDOM

English Channel

BELGIUM

GERMANY

LUXEMBOURG

■ Paris

Strasbourg ○

Can you find out which two tiny countries France also **borders?**

○ Nantes

**FRANCE**

SWITZERLAND

Atlantic Ocean

○ Lyon

ITALY

○ Bordeaux

Bayonne ○

Nice

Cannes ○○

○ Biarritz

○ Toulouse

Marseille ○

**Corsica**

SPAIN

Mediterranean Sea

France

**EUROPE**

Paris is the **capital** city of France. More than 2 million people live there. It has many famous museums, art galleries, churches and other old buildings.

The Eiffel Tower is one of Paris's most well-known sights. It was built around 125 years ago, and since then 250 million people have climbed it!

FACT CAT FACT

France is the most visited country in the world. Every year, more than 80 million **tourists** travel there.

# CITIES

Paris is the largest city in France. Marseille, Lyon, Toulouse, Nice and Nantes are the next five biggest cities. They all have very different weather, food and **traditions**.

Marseille is on the south coast, and is often hot and sunny. Many people from North Africa live there, and make traditional North African food and music.

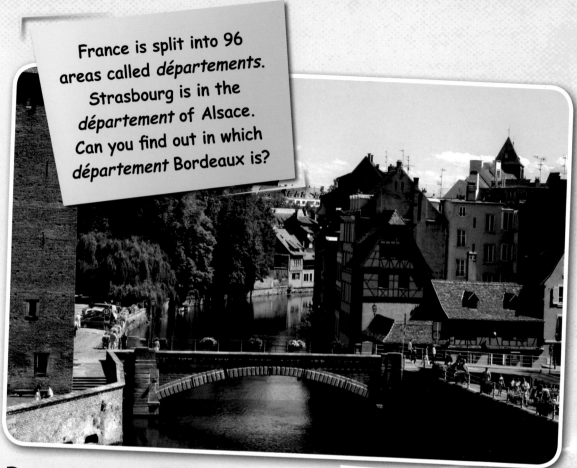

France is split into 96 areas called *départements*. Strasbourg is in the *département* of Alsace. Can you find out in which *département* Bordeaux is?

France has more than 800 cities and towns. There are large cities all over the country, from Strasbourg in the north-east to Bordeaux in the south-west.

Strasbourg is very close to France's border with Germany. The city has not always been part of France. At times in the past, it was part of Germany.

# COUNTRYSIDE

A lot of France's land is used for farming. Farmers around the country grow many different **crops**, such as **wheat**, potatoes, tomatoes, apples, grapes and **sunflowers**.

Farmers in the south-east often grow lavender flowers. They make soap smell nice, and can also be used in food. Try to find a recipe that includes lavender.

France has different types of landscape. Some areas have lots of mountains, and others have grassy plains or large forests. Many people live in villages or small towns in the countryside.

Farmers keep animals such as sheep, goats, chickens, cows and geese. These sheep live on a farm in the Pyrénées Mountains.

**FACT CAT FACT**

French adults tell children stories about a wild mountain animal called a dahu. They say it looks like a goat, but it has two shorter legs on one side of its body. This means it can walk easily around the steep mountain slopes.

# COAST AND ISLANDS

France has a very long coast. Some parts are rocky, with high cliffs and stony beaches. Other parts have long, wide sandy beaches.

Mont St Michel is a small island just off the north-west coast. It has a large **abbey** built around 500 years ago. Only 44 people live on the island.

The south of France is hotter and drier than the north. Many French people spend their holidays in southern seaside towns such as Cannes and Biarritz.

**FACT CAT FACT**

Some parts of France are very far away from the rest of the country. La Réunion is a French island off the coast of **Madagascar**. It is more than 9000 km (5600 miles) away from mainland France!

Corsica is a French island off the south-east coast. It is closer to another country than it is to **mainland France**. Can you find out which country?

# FOOD

France is famous for its cheese, bread and cakes. More than 600 types of cheese are made in France. The cheeses contain milk from cows, sheep or goats.

**Macarons** are sweet French treats that come in many colours and flavours. You can eat raspberry, chocolate or even carrot and orange macarons!

Different areas of France have their own traditional dishes. Cassoulet is a popular southern **stew** made with beans and meat. Choucroute garnie is a northern dish of cabbage, potatoes and sausage.

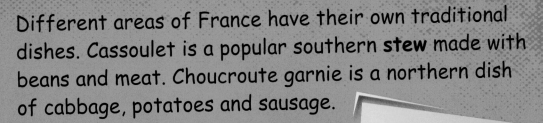

One traditional French dish is snails cooked in garlic butter. Can you find out what this dish is called in French?

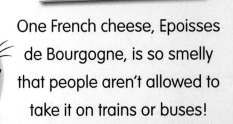

## FACT CAT FACT

One French cheese, Epoisses de Bourgogne, is so smelly that people aren't allowed to take it on trains or buses!

# WILDLIFE

A wide range of animals live in different areas across France. There are 240 types of butterfly, and 120 different **mammals** such as deer, **beavers** and **wild boar**.

The common genet lives in the forests, **scrubland** and rocky areas of France. Can you find out which other countries it lives in?

Lots of animals live in and around the Alps, a long mountain range that runs through part of France. They include **chamois**, golden eagles, **pine martens** and wolves.

## FACT CAT FACT

It can get very cold in the Alps, and at these times there is not much food for larger animals. The Alpine marmot eats a lot in the summer, and then goes into a deep sleep for the other nine months of the year.

# FESTIVALS AND HOLIDAYS

Many festivals are celebrated in different areas of France. The Fêtes de Bayonne is the country's largest festival. More than 1 million people take part every August.

The Fêtes de Bayonne celebrates the traditional culture of the Basque region. This is an area that is part of both France and Spain.

France has many holidays throughout the year. Bastille Day is France's national day. It is celebrated on June 14, with fireworks and **parades**.

Mardi Gras is another popular French holiday. People wear costumes and have big street parties. Can you find out what day Mardi Gras takes place this year?

## FACT CAT FACT

In English, 'Mardi Gras' means 'Fat Tuesday'. In the past, many people gave up rich food for forty days before Easter. Mardi Gras was the last day before this began, so people used up all their sugar and butter to make delicious foods!

# SPORT

Football is the most popular sport in France. Many people also enjoy playing and watching tennis, rugby, basketball and **handball**.

Thierry Henry is a famous French football player. He has scored more goals for France than any other player in history.

Other popular sports in France are cycling, **skiing** and **Pétanque**. The Tour de France is a famous cycling race that is held every year.

Tour de France cyclists travel around 3200 km (2000 miles) over 21 days. Can you find out when the first Tour de France took place?

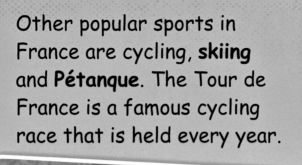

**FACT CAT FACT**

Every year, around 15 million people come to stand along the race route and watch the Tour de France. That is almost seven times more people than live in Paris!

# FAMOUS PEOPLE

There are many famous French people in history. Napoleon Bonaparte was the leader of France around 200 years ago, and he fought many battles against other countries.

After Napoleon lost the Battle of Waterloo against Britain, he was forced to live on an island off the coast of Africa. What was the island's name?

## FACT CAT FACT

Many people today believe that Napoleon was very short. In fact, he was average height for a man.

Marie Curie was a famous French scientist. She discovered that some materials give off invisible **rays**. These rays are called radiation, and can be dangerous.

Marie Curie was the first person to win two **Nobel Prizes**, and the first woman to ever win one at all. Her daughter Irène also won a Nobel Prize.

**QUIZ**

Try to answer the questions below. Look back through the book to help you. Check your answers on page 24.

**1** Marseille is the largest city in France. True or not true?

a) true

b) not true

**2** In which part of France is the town of Cannes?

a) north

b) west

c) south

**3** What type of race is the Tour de France?

a) running race

b) cycling race

c) swimming race

**4** What is cassoulet?

a) a stew made with beans and meat

b) a city in central France

c) a brown, furry animal

**5** Marie Curie was the first person to ever win a Nobel Prize. True or not true?

a) true

b) not true

**6** How many types of cheese are made in France?

a) 80

b) 12

c) more than 600

# GLOSSARY

**abbey** building where religious people called monks and nuns live

**beaver** animal that has long front teeth and a wide, flat tail

**border** to be next to something

**capital** the city where the government (the group of people that leads a country) meets

**chamois** animal that looks like a goat and lives in the mountains

**crops** plants that are grown for food

**handball** game in which players use their hands to hit a ball against a wall

**macaron** two pieces of meringue, which is a light, crunchy dessert made from eggs and sugar, with flavoured cream or jam in the middle

**Madagascar** island country off the south-east coast of Africa

**mainland** the main area of a country

**mammal** a type of animal, often with fur, that feeds its babies milk

**Nobel Prize** special award that is given to a person who does great work in science, mathematics and other subjects

**parade** group of people moving together along a street to celebrate something

**Pétanque** game in which players try to throw metal balls as close as possible to a small wooden ball

**pine marten** animal that has a long, narrow body with mostly dark brown fur

**ray** straight line of light or heat

**scrubland** land that is covered with low, rough plants, bushes and trees

**skiing** sport in which people slide down mountains with each of their feet on a long, narrow piece of plastic

**stew** dish that is cooked slowly in one pot until the ingredients are soft

**sunflower** tall plant with large, yellow flowers

**tourist** someone who visits a place on holiday

**tradition** something that a group of people has done the same way for a long time

**wheat** plant with parts that can be used to make flour for bread or cakes

**wild boar** type of pig that lives in the forest

23

# INDEX

# ANSWERS

## Pages 4–20

**page 4:** Monaco and Andorra

**page 7:** Gironde

**page 11:** Italy

**page 13:** Escargots à la Bourguignonne

**page 14:** Spain, Portugal, most countries in Africa and some countries in the Middle East (a small number have been found in Germany, Belgium and Switzerland, but they probably escaped from homes or zoos/wildlife parks)

**page 19:** 1 July, 1903

**page 20:** Saint Helena

## Quiz answers

1  b) Not true. Paris is the largest city in France.

2  c) south

3  b) cycling race

4  a) a stew made with beans and meat

5  b) Not true. She was the first person to ever win two Nobel Prizes, and the first woman to ever win a Nobel Prize.

6  c) more than 600

# OTHER TITLES IN THE FACT CAT SERIES...

## SPACE

**THE EARTH**

978 0 7502 8220 8

**THE MOON**

978 0 7502 8221 5

**THE PLANETS**

978 0 7502 8222 2

**THE SUN**

978 0 7502 8223 9

## UNITED KINGDOM

978 0 7502 8433 2

**ENGLAND**

**NORTHERN IRELAND**

978 0 7502 8440 0

978 0 7502 8439 4

**SCOTLAND**

**WALES**

978 0 7502 8438 7

## HISTORY

**AMELIA EARHART**
Transatlantic Pilot

978 0 7502 9034 0

978 0 7502 9037 1

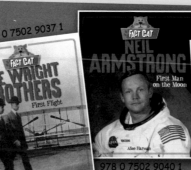

**THE WRIGHT BROTHERS**
First Flight

**NEIL ARMSTRONG**
First Man on the Moon

978 0 7502 9040 1

978 0 7502 9031 9

**CHRISTOPHER COLUMBUS**
Discovering America

WAYLAND